Every Day is
A Gift

A Journey of the Heart

By

Sue Schmig

Sue Schmig

DEDICATION

To my husband, Tim, who encouraged me to write this book and who was patient with me even though it took me eight years to do it, and who was firm with me when he knew it was time. He was with me every step of the way throughout my journey with breast cancer and showed all of us what it is like to love in sickness and in health. Thank you Tim. You are my true hero and I love you more than I can say.

And to the millions of people that have walked through the "valley of the shadow of death" with cancer, you are some of my heroes. I know what you have been through and I know what you have felt and what you have thought. I trust you have learned, like I have, that Every Day is A Gift!

INTRODUCTION

On Good Friday, 2010 I found out I had breast cancer and it had also spread into some of my lymph nodes. This is my story of the journey God placed me on in March of 2010. The pages that follow are from a blog I created on social media. I started journaling because it was therapeutic for me. As I began to write and share what God was doing I also began praying that my writings would be a blessing and encouragement to those who were reading. Many people have shared with me how God answered that prayer and used my blog to encourage them. It is my desire that God would use this book in a great way to bless, encourage, help and inspire many, and perhaps rebuke some who may need rebuking. This book is filled with answers to prayer that God gave to me as I was going through my journey with breast cancer. It is also filled with lessons that God taught me along the way and Scriptures that he gave to me to encourage me as I was seeking Him and trying to learn what He was teaching me. I have learned that God brings trials of all sorts into our lives to draw us close to Him. A correct response would be to draw close to Him. My choice was to obey and draw close to Him. What a wonderful place that is! He gave me joy, peace, grace and calm. Peace in the midst of my storm. God always brings trials into our lives for our own good and for His own glory. We must choose to find the good and give Him the glory. I have also learned how important it is to make every detail of our lives a matter of prayer and to be thankful in every situation we find ourselves in. God has a plan for each of our lives and sometimes that plan includes things that we would never have planned for ourselves, like cancer. I can say I am thankful that God allowed me to have cancer because He taught me things that I could not have learned any other way.

"Be careful for nothing; but in every thing by prayer and supplication with thanksgiving let your requests be made known unto God. And the peace of God, which passeth all understanding, shall keep your hearts and minds through Christ Jesus." Philippians 4: 6 & 7

Sue Schmig

Topic of Cancer

Denial.

"This can't be happening to us, cancer happens to other people, this can't be happening." So I voiced my first attempt to comprehend the journey Sue and I began on Good Friday 2010.

Making our way back to our home, lost in thought, my mind racing through 'what if' scenarios, I felt numb. I know people talk about having an out-of-body experience, seeing themselves in third person, observing their life instead of living it, I guess that's where I was.

Sue and I sat through that evening praying, talking, thinking and weeping until I just couldn't go on any longer, I was spent, wrung out, emotionally and physically exhausted. I went to bed. A couple of hours later Sue made her way to bed and we tossed and turned until about midnight and I said "Let's go to the family room and read our Bibles". We read Psalms to each other, hearing the Word of God through the voice of human experience in the life of King David and others. Long into our reading Sue looked at me and with a calm voice said "I feel a peace come over me." I replied, "Do you know why that is?" When the disciples were leaving the Lord in his ministry he turned to the inner circle of Peter, James and John and said, 'Will you leave me also?' 'To whom shall we go? Thou hast the words of life.' God's Word is alive and powerful and able to calm the most troubled heart.

This is Sue's story. I was blessed to be able to be a part of it and to be there every step of the way. The reality of it is, Sue had cancer, she took the chemo, she had the surgery. It was amazing and humbling to watch her walk each day in full faith, nothing wavering and inspire others with her cheerfulness. I often think that the blessing of this cancer was that it gave me a second chance to take inventory of my life and try to live my life in a more caring and compassionate way. I'm a different person for having walked with Sue on this journey. Coming face to face with our own frailty and mortality will do that to us.

We could never fully thank everyone who encouraged us on this journey. To this day I am often asked "How is Sue doing"? A few people come to mind that I would be remiss to not acknowledge. Dr. Mark Rasmussen at West Coast Baptist Bible College. Many weeks he sent Sue a card of encouragement. Every week Jay & Debbie, gave us ionized water to help Sue stay hydrated and it worked wonders. A man in our church faithfully brought us herbal tea for comfort and encouragement. I need to thank all of you who prayed and still have us on your daily prayer list, Edd, Bobby & Betty you are a constant encouragement. Thank you.

--Tim Schmig

APRIL 5, 2010

My immediate family and my Faith Baptist Church family know that I have cancer and now I need to share with the rest of my friends. Last Wednesday, March 31, I had a core biopsy of my right breast and lymph node under my right arm. I received the pathology report late Friday afternoon that I do have breast cancer and it has already spread into my lymph nodes. Because of changing insurance companies recently I also had to find a new doctor that would accept our new insurance. The Lord provided in a great way and this afternoon I was able to get in to see my new doctor who advised that I should have surgery within the next couple of weeks. Chemotherapy will follow sometime about six or seven weeks after my surgery. It is amazing how fast your life can change in one day, and what a shock the news of cancer can be, but I am so thankful that this was not a surprise to my Heavenly Father and what a comfort it is to know it is all a part of His plan for my life right now. I am trusting Him to carry me through and I know whatever happens it will be for my good and His glory. My doctor told us today this is an "aggressive and angry" cancer but the good news is that aggressive cancers are aggressively treated. Please pray that this cancer would not have spread anywhere else and that all the rest of the test results would be coming back negative. I should find out tomorrow when my appointment for my MRI will be and also my appointment with my surgeon. Thank you so much to those of you who have been praying for me. I would like to share some verses that have been a great comfort to me these past few days.

Psalm 61:2 *"From the end of the earth will I cry unto thee, when my heart is overwhelmed: lead me to the rock that is higher than I."*

Psalm 62:8 *"Trust in him at all times; ye people, pour out your heart before him: God is a refuge for us."*

Psalm 46:1 *"God is our refuge and strength, a very present help in trouble."*

Phil. 4:6 *"Be anxious for nothing; but in everything by prayer and supplication with thanksgiving let your requests be made known unto God. And the peace of God which passeth all understanding shall keep your hearts and minds through Christ Jesus."*

I have cried out to God for his help and He is ever faithful. I can say God has given me a peace in my heart that I know only He can give and I know it is because so many people are praying for me. I ask for your continued prayers in the days and months ahead. I don't know what lies ahead for me, but I know God knows, so it is ok. God is always good!

APRIL 6, 2010

Thank you, dear friends, for the many notes, messages, phone calls and prayers. What an encouragement to my heart you have been. I am going to use this space to journal my journey with breast cancer over the next several months. It is therapy for me and it is my prayer that it will be an encouragement, in some small way to you, should you choose to read along. Of course I am praying for complete healing, but if God has other plans for me it is ok. He always knows best and I am fully aware that God does not always choose to heal those who have cancer. He may have a better plan. Sometimes, in His providence He will choose to call His dear ones home through cancer. His plan and His way is always best.

After I received my pathology report I spent most of Friday evening on the phone calling my girls, my sister, my mom, my dad, my mother and father-in-law, a dear friend. What a hard thing to tell your loved ones you have cancer and then not be able to see them or hug them because they are so far away. (Tim and Hannah, I am so thankful you are here with me every day and that we can encourage each other during this time!) In some small way I felt guilty telling them because I knew it would hurt them. They were hurting for me. I want them to know that I am ok because I know God has a purpose in all of this. I don't know everything that purpose involves yet, but I am excited to find out. I do know that I want to bring glory to Him through this journey.

In some ways this doesn't even seem real to me yet. I have no pain, I'm still getting up and going to work every day, I have lots of energy, I don't look any different, but I know someday very soon this is going to change. My doctor told me yesterday I will probably be getting a new hairdo....... But I do want to be changed. I want to love God more. I want to know Him in a deeper way. I want to learn what He wants me to learn while on this journey. What an opportunity God has given to me and I don't want to waste it. The February 15, 2006 article by John Piper entitled, "Don't Waste Your Cancer"[1] has been a great blessing to me. He says "I believe in God's power to heal--by miracle and by medicine. I believe it is right and good to pray for both kinds of healing. Cancer is not wasted when it is healed by God. He gets the glory and that is why cancer exists. So, not to pray for healing may waste your cancer. But healing is not God's plan for everyone. And there are many other ways to waste your cancer. I am praying for myself and for you that we will not waste this pain." Today I will share his first point:

1." You will waste your cancer if you do not believe it is designed for you by God."

"It will not do to say that God only uses our cancer but does not design it. What God permits, he permits for a reason. And that reason is his design. If God foresees molecular developments becoming cancer, he can stop it or not. If he does not, he has a purpose. Since he is infinitely wise, it is right to call this purpose a design. Satan is real and causes many pleasures and pains. But he is not ultimate. So when he strikes Job with boils (Job 2:7), Job attributes it ultimately to God (2:10) and the inspired writer agrees: "They...comforted him over all the evil that the Lord had brought upon him" (Job 42:11). If you don't believe your cancer is

---

[1] Don't Waste Your Cancer by John Piper www.desiringgod.org February, 2006

designed for you by God, you will waste it."

I am scheduled to have my MRI this Thursday at 8:30 am. The next appointment will be meeting my surgeon on Monday, April 12. I am praying that I will go away from that appointment knowing my surgery date. We would like to have my surgery as soon as possible. Our family has many things scheduled for this spring/summer including a trip to Maranatha Baptist Bible College for Baccalaureate/Commencement the first weekend in May. Then Hannah's wedding the last weekend in May followed the next week by a trip to Wilmington, NC to visit with Rebekah and see her kindergarten class graduate. Then at the end of July we planned to go to Alaska to be with my mom for her 90th birthday party. God knows about all of this and we are trusting Him because our plans may not be what He has planned. Right now I need to take one day at a time and focus on what He wants me to do today. Taking one day at a time is so important when you are going through a life trial. In "The Lord's Prayer," Jesus instructs us to focus on "this day." "Give us this day our daily bread." Matthew 6:11 He does not ask for provisions for tomorrow or next week, but for this day. Lord, please help me to trust you for what I need today.

This evening I called my friend, Carolyn, who lives in South Carolina. We have been friends for nearly 30 years. We got married around the same time, went to the same church, lived next to each other in the same apartment complex, had our first babies at the same time. Fast friends. Faithful friends. Carolyn was diagnosed with lymphoma in her lungs last November. She has had chemo and is doing some better, but she is still living with cancer. I have been praying for her every day since I found out about this journey she is on. Now we share something else.

Please pray for my friend Carolyn. Her type of cancer is slow growing and she may require some other form of treatment down the road. Tonight I told her I have breast cancer and now she knows how to pray for me.

These verses have been of great comfort to me: Psalm 73:25 & 26 *"Whom have I in heaven but thee? and there is none upon earth that I desire beside thee. My flesh and my heart faileth but God is the strength of my heart and my portion forever."*

Thank you again all who are praying.

APRIL 8, 2010

"I had fainted, unless I had believed to see the goodness of the Lord in the land of the living. Wait on the Lord: be of good courage, and he shall strengthen thine heart: wait, I say, on the Lord." Psalm 27:13-14

I am so blessed to have so many people praying for me and begging God to bring healing and comfort. To simply say "thank you" seems way too inadequate. I feel your love and prayers and for that I am so grateful. Many of you have shared special verses with me that have been an encouragement to you during a time of trial or testing in your life. I received the verses I just quoted from a godly lady friend in an email this morning. What an encouragement these verses are to me as now I am waiting. Waiting to see my surgeon on Monday with the results of the MRI I had today. Waiting for a surgery date and to know the exact type of surgery I will have. Waiting to know if my cancer is anywhere else in my body. God tells me to be of good courage and he will strengthen me. How can I get discouraged when I read that? Thank you Lord for your Word that comforts me when I feel weary and discouraged.

The MRI I had today was of my chest area only. More scans of my entire body will be done after surgery.

Let me tell you of how God has already answered some of your prayers for me. On Friday after I learned that I had breast cancer, I was without a doctor. I had to change to a doctor that would accept our insurance since we had recently changed insurance companies and the doctor I had been going to for the past ten years did not accept our new insurance. We prayed earnestly over the weekend that God would lead us and direct us to the doctor he wanted me to have. I really wanted to see Dr. N but I knew she was not accepting new patients now. I thought she would probably see me one time and recommend someone to me. We were going to go to her office around 11:00 on Monday morning to see if we could talk with her. Dr. N called me on my cell phone Monday morning around 9:30 before we ever went to her office to say she wanted to help me. I expressed my thanks and said I knew she wasn't taking any new patients now, but maybe she could recommend someone to me. Then she said, "no, I want to help you. I will be your doctor if you want me to." Praise God! I told her I would love for her to be my doctor. She had me come in to see her that very afternoon! I am so thankful to have a doctor that calls me at home to see how I am doing. She prays for us and she treats us like family. She has directed us to a surgeon who she trusted enough to have operate on her own family members. I am thankful she is aggressive in the way she wants to treat this cancer. That is what we prayed for. God is already answering prayers!

I also had another great blessing this week when I learned that two friends are going to be running in a 5K race on May 22 to raise money to fight breast cancer. They are running the race in my honor. When I read the message from my friend telling me of their plans, all I could do was cry because I was so deeply touched and overwhelmed with love.

I am so excited that Sarah is coming home from Tennessee this weekend! She and Mike's Aunt are driving up so they can go to a family bridal shower on Saturday. They will leave around 4:00 p.m. Friday evening and drive through until they get in and should be here around 2:00 a.m. Saturday. Please pray for their safety as they travel. Sarah has said she is going to stay here with us until after my surgery and we are thankful she can do that. God provided a new job for her recently (she was not looking for a new job, but God brought it to her) and she works from home now. As long as she has her computer she can work anywhere, so she will be bringing her computer with her and working here for a few weeks. God did that for Sarah and for us in our time of need. Jehovahjireh! God provides!

Getting back to the article "Don't Waste Your Cancer,"[2] I want to share the second point:

2." You will waste your cancer if you believe it is a curse and not a gift."

"There is therefore now no condemnation to them which are in Christ Jesus" (Romans 8:1). "Christ hath redeemed us from the curse of the law, being made a curse for us" (Galatians 3:13). "Surely there is no enchantment against Jacob, neither is there any divination against Israel" (Numbers 23:23). "For the Lord God is a sun and shield; the Lord will give grace and glory: no good thing will he withhold from them that walk uprightly" (Psalm 84:11).

I believe my cancer is a gift and not a curse. He has given me this gift to share with others what he is doing in my life. Philippians 2:13, *"For it is God which worketh in you both to will and to do of his good pleasure."* My cancer was no coincidence, but was always part of God's plan for me. He organized each detail

---

[2] Ibid.

including where I would be living, what doctors I would have and what hospital I would have my surgery. Since God planned this for me it could never be a curse because God only does things for our good and for His glory. Just because something in our life is unpleasant or uncomfortable does not mean it is a curse. All of us have troubles in life. Job says in Job 5:7, *"Yet man is born unto trouble, as the sparks fly upward."* Please pray that I would not waste my cancer, but that I would take every opportunity I get to tell others what God is doing through me because of this gift He has given to me.

APRIL 11, 2010

Two things I am so thankful for today: Grace and Peace.

"And he said unto me, my grace is sufficient for thee: for my strength is made perfect in weakness. Most gladly therefore will I rather glory in my infirmities that the power of Christ may rest upon me." II Corinthians 12:9

"For he is our peace" Eph. 2:14

"And the peace of God which passeth all understanding shall keep your hearts and minds through Christ Jesus." Phil 4:7

"And let the peace of God rule in your hearts, to the which also ye are called in one body; and be ye thankful." Col 3:15

My heart is blessed to have been told by so many of you that you are praying for me every day. What an encouragement that is to me. Please know that I can feel your prayers for me because God has given me such a peace in my heart. He is helping me to trust and not to fear. My God is so much bigger than any challenge I face!

This passage of scripture in Mark 4 where Jesus calms the storm at sea has been a blessing to me many times, but recently has become so precious to me. Verse 36 *says "And when they had sent away the multitude, they took him even as he was in the ship. And there were also with him other little ships."* What a comfort to know that when we go through the storms of life, Jesus is right there in the ship with us! There were other little ships on that sea that day, but Jesus was not in those ships. I am so thankful I have the Lord in my heart to comfort me as I go through this storm. I don't know what I would do without Him, and I don't know what the lost world does when they go through storms of life.

Here is the next point from the article "Don't Waste Your Cancer"[3] by John Piper:

3. "You will waste your cancer if you seek comfort from your odds rather than from God."

"The design of God in your cancer is not to train you in the rationalistic, human calculation of odds. The world gets comfort from their odds. Not Christians. Some count their chariots (percentages of survival) and some count their horses (side effects of treatment), but we trust in the name of the Lord our God (Psalm 20:7). God's design is clear from 2 Corinthians 1:9 - 'We felt that we had received the sentence of death. But that was to make us rely not on ourselves but on God who raises the dead.' The aim of God in your cancer (among a thousand other good things) is to knock props out from under our hearts so that we rely utterly on him. God himself is your comfort. He gives himself. The hymn "Be Still My Soul" reckons the odds the right way: we are 100% certain to suffer, and Christ is 100% certain to meet us, to come for us, comfort us, and restore love's purest joys. The hymn "How Firm a Foundation" reckons the odds the same way: you are 100% certain to pass through grave distresses, and your Savior is 100% certain to 'be with you, your troubles to bless, and sanctify to you your deepest distress.' With God, you aren't

---

[3] Ibid.

playing percentages, but living within certainties."

I had the great blessing tonight to listen to a man in our church give a testimony of how God healed him of his cancer! He has battled this disease for almost two years now. The doctors had almost given up on him and God took his cancer away and today he is cancer free. Praise God! We know that with God all things are possible, even when the odds are against us!

Please pray for my appointment with my surgeon, Dr. V, tomorrow at 3:45. He will be talking to us about the results of my MRI that I had on Thursday. Please pray that I would be able to have my surgery as soon as possible. Also please pray for me to be a testimony to Dr. V.

Thank you for all who are praying.

APRIL 12, 2010

Just a quick note to say no surgery date yet. We have some important decisions to make over the next few days. I will be having some more tests this week before a decision can be made. Please pray for God's leading and direction and for wisdom to know what is best for me.

The MRI results were good in that there was no other cancer seen in the chest area other than what showed up on the mammogram and ultrasound. Thank you so much for praying.

APRIL 13, 2010

"Call unto me, and I will answer thee, and shew thee great and mighty things, which thou knowest not." Jeremiah 33:3

After meeting with my surgeon yesterday, he wanted me to have more testing done to be sure the cancer had not spread into other areas of my body. It is not uncommon for this type of cancer to travel to the lymph nodes (which it already has), the liver, the lungs, the bones and the brain. Today at 1:30 I had an appointment for a CAT scan of my chest, abdomen and pelvic areas. Before 5:00 this afternoon Dr. N called me with the news that no cancer was seen in any of those areas. Praise the Lord! This is a huge answer to prayer! Tomorrow I go for bone scans. I have to go in at 9:00 for an injection and then go back at noon when they will actually do the bone scans. Then I meet again late tomorrow afternoon with my surgeon and he will go over all those results with me. Thank you so much for all your prayers for me!

I want to share the words to a song that I have been singing in my head this week. I didn't know all the words until today. The song is entitled, "Grace," by Carolyn Hamlin, and has been a great blessing to me.

Lord, as I seek Your guidance for the day
I find my thoughts unyielding, confusion crowds my way.
But then when I bow to You, the challenges You guide me through.
Your promises are ever new; I claim them for today.

Chorus:
Your will cannot lead me where Your grace will not keep me.
Your hands will protect me; I rest in Your care.
Your eyes will watch over me, Your love will forgive me.
And when I am faltering, I still will find You there.

Each new day's design is charted by Your hands
And graciously revealed as I seek Your master plan.
Keep my footsteps faithful when from You I go;
Return me to the joy that Your blessings can bestow.

Tim and I just got home from evangelistic services at Community
Baptist Church in Saginaw where Brother Hal Hightower is
preaching this week. It was "School Night" and what a blessing to
hear both the elementary kids and Jr. High/High School kids
singing special music, and then Brother Hightower preached a
great message. My heart is full and so blessed tonight!

APRIL 14, 2010

We met with the surgeon late this afternoon and he told us the bone scans I had today were negative as well as the CAT scan I had yesterday!

I want to sing and shout! *"It is a good thing to give thanks unto the Lord, and to sing praises unto thy name, O most High:"* Psalm 92:1

The next thing is for me to meet with my oncologist. I have an appointment with him next Wednesday, but we are trying to get in to see him yet this week. Please pray that that would be possible and that it would happen. I should know about that sometime tomorrow morning.

Thank you so much for all your encouraging words and for your prayers for me and for our family. I can't tell you what an encouragement it is to us to know you are praying.

God is so good!

APRIL 15, 2010

God has answered another prayer for us today and for that we are so thankful. I was able to get in to see my oncologist, Dr. A, this afternoon. We had prayed about this and decided that whatever course of action he wanted us to pursue, we would do, whether that meant having surgery first and then chemo, or chemo first and then surgery. Dr. V, the surgeon had suggested possibly having chemo first and before he suggested that, I had not even given that a thought. I thought surgery would come first. Well when we met Dr. A today and he recommended starting chemo right away. Even though the CAT scan and bone scans came back clear, he said with the cancer that I have that is so aggressive and fast growing there could still be cancer cells other places in my body that the tests did not pick up and because of that they want to begin chemo as soon as possible. Before that can happen I have to have a heart scan to be sure my heart is strong enough to endure the chemo. That test will be done on Monday. Then I will have a port inserted in my chest and that will stay in throughout the twenty four weeks of chemo. Depending on when I get the port put in, I could start chemo as early as Tuesday or Wednesday of next week. The chemo will be given once every three weeks for the first twelve weeks and then once a week for twelve more weeks. Surgery will come after that and then radiation (possibly) after that.

I had planned that I would have surgery right away and be healed up in time to make the trip to Maranatha on May 5 and be feeling great for Hannah & Kyle's wedding. Then chemo would start after we got back from Wilmington the first part of June.....My plans are not always what God has planned for me. I will not ask why, I will only trust that He knows what is best for me. We believe God led us to these doctors and we are trusting them to provide the best possible care and treatment for me. As we walked into the cancer treatment center, reality hit me square in the face as I looked around and saw people being treated for their cancer. I saw sick, bald people. Before, it didn't quite seem real to me. Now it is beginning to seem all too real that I do have cancer. What an opportunity God has given to me to be able to talk with so many of these good doctors and nurses who work in oncology. As we shook Dr. A's hand as he was leaving I told him we had been praying for him. I told him we were Christians and gave him a Gospel tract to read just as I had done for Dr. V after our first meeting with him. Then as one of the nurses who was walking us out was saying goodbye to us I handed her a tract, asked her if she could read it and then we could talk about it the next time I saw her. Please pray for boldness for me as I try and be a witness and share my faith with those I come in contact with at the Cancer Institute over the next twenty four weeks. Pray that I won't waste one opportunity.

Here is the 4th point in John Piper's article entitled "Don't Waste Your Cancer:"[4]

4. "You will waste your cancer if you refuse to think about death."

"We all die, if Jesus postpones his return. Not to think about what it will be like to leave this life and meet God is folly. Ecclesiastes 7:2 says, 'It is better to go to the house of mourning [a funeral] than to go to the house of feasting, for that is the end of all men, and the living will lay it to his heart.' How can you lay it to heart if you won't think about it? Psalm 90:12 says, 'So teach us to

---

[4] Ibid

number our days that we may apply our hearts unto wisdom.'
Numbering your days means thinking about how few there are
and that they will end. How will you get a heart of wisdom if you
refuse to think about this? What a waste, if we do not think about
death. Paul describes the Holy Spirit as the unseen, inner
'downpayment' on the certainty of life. By faith, the Lord gives a
sweet taste of the face-to-face reality of eternal life in the
presence of our God and Christ. We might also say that cancer is
one 'downpayment' on inevitable death, giving one bad taste of
the reality of our mortality. Cancer is a signpost pointing to
something far bigger: the last enemy that you must face. But
Christ has defeated this last enemy: 1 Corinthians 15. Death is
swallowed up in victory. Cancer is merely one of the enemy's
scouting parties, out on patrol. It has no final power if you are a
child of the resurrection, so you can look it in the eye."

I am not afraid of what is ahead for me. I know God is going with
me. I plan on having a lot more living to do. Tim and I still have a
whole lot more places where we want to travel. We have places
to see and things to do! Connecticut, North Carolina and
Tennessee sound like some great places to visit!

Let me close with a verse that the Lord gave to me this morning.
*"The Lord is my light and my salvation; whom shall I fear? the Lord
is the strength of my life, of whom shall I be afraid?"* Psalm 27:1
Because of Him, I have no need to fear. "How can I fear, Jesus is
near, He ever watches over me. Worries all cease, He gives me
peace. How can I fear with Jesus?"

Thank you so much for all your care, concern and prayers! God is
good!

APRIL 17, 2010

What a surprise we had today! Hannah left tonight to go out for dinner with friends (wink, wink!) and she returned home about an hour later with Rebekah!! She came home from Wilmington, NC to surprise us and will be here until Wednesday. We are so thankful to have her here with us at this time. Some very generous people provided her with an airline ticket. They saw a need and met it and for that we are so very thankful!

Just a quick update on what is happening this week. On Monday I will have a heart scan to be sure my heart is strong enough to endure the chemo, and will also have my port put in. My surgeon, Dr. V, will do that procedure. Then on Tuesday I will start my chemo. Please pray that the treatments will be effective, that the side effects will be minimal and that I will be able to work as much as possible throughout the treatments that will last twenty four weeks.

These words from Andrew Murray have been an inspiration to me:
"First, He brought me here. It is by His will I am in this strait place: in that fact I will rest.
Next, He will keep me here in His love, and give me grace to behave as His child.
Then, He will make the trial a blessing, teaching me the lessons He intends me to learn, and working in me the grace He means to bestow.
Last, in His good time He can bring me out again - how and when He knows.

Let me say I am here,

1) By God's appointment,
2) In His Keeping,
3) Under His training,
4) For His time."
- Andrew Murray[5]

God has given me incredible grace and peace and I believe it is because of the power of your prayers for me. I pray I will learn the lessons He intends me to learn while on this journey. Thank you so much for all of your prayers! God is so good!

Just before my first chemo treatment.

---

[5] Andrew Murray: Christ's Anointed Minister to South Africa

APRIL 19, 2010

Thank you all so much for your prayers for me today. We arrived at the hospital at 7:15 and met Dr. V in the hallway as we were walking up to check in. He made us feel so comfortable about the procedure and Rebekah & Hannah got to meet him today. The surgery was scheduled for 9:15 and was right on schedule. It took quite a bit longer that what they told us and by the time I got out of recovery and had something to eat it was 12:40. My heart scan was scheduled for 1:00 in Fenton, so we went right over there from the hospital. That went well also and we got back home a little after 3:00 this afternoon. Naps for all of the girls followed! Then we enjoyed a relaxing evening here with a friend who brought dinner over for us. Thank you, Carolyn! We love you!

After my nap I came downstairs to read my Bible and the Lord had me turn to Psalm 16. What a great chapter that begins with *"Preserve me, O God: for in thee do I put my trust"* and ends with *"Thou wilt shew me the path of life: in thy presence is fulness of joy; at thy right hand there are pleasures for evermore."* And then in Chapter 17:8 *"Keep me as the apple of the eye, hide me under the shadow of thy wings."* God is my protector and what a great place to hide! Such a comfort!

Tomorrow I start my chemo at 1:00. All my family will be with me there and I feel so blessed to be surrounded with their love and support. Tim, Sarah, Rebekah and Hannah I love you more than you could ever know. Thank you for being here for me.

I am feeling well tonight and enjoying every minute of it! Please continue to pray.

APRIL 20, 2010

Just a quick note to let everyone know I am doing really well so far after my first treatment. The treatment went well--a little longer than we thought. We were there until almost 5:00. All five of us were there and what a comfort it was to have my family so near me today. I am so thankful for my family. We came home and ate dinner and then Rebekah and I went for a walk outside. I'm feeling great as of 9:00 pm tonight! I know all your prayers for me are carrying me through this day. I am very thankful also for the medicine I can take to prevent/help nausea! I don't know what tomorrow or the next day will bring, but I know God will be with me helping me through. He is always good.

It has been so wonderful having Rebekah home for a few days. She will fly out late tomorrow morning. Please pray for a safe trip home for her. I know it will be difficult for all of us to say goodbye, but, we will see her again in just a few weeks!

This is a verse my mom sent me in an email a few days ago: *"Trust in him at all times; ye people, pour out your heart before him: God is a refuge for us."* Psalm 62:8 Thank you, Mom. I love you!

APRIL 24, 2010

"Fear not, for I have redeemed thee, I have called thee by thy name; thou art mine! When thou passest through the waters, I wilt be with thee; and through the rivers, they shall not overflow thee: when thou walkest through the fire, thou shalt not be burned; neither shall the flame kindle upon thee. For I am the LORD thy God." Isaiah 43: 1-3

One chemo treatment down, fifteen more to go! Never having gone down this path before, I really did not know what to expect, since everyone is different. I am so thankful that I really did not experience much sickness at all, but rather, extreme tiredness. In fact, I could barely keep my eyes open for two whole days! God gave me wonderful sleep, and that is just what my body needed! I am still feeling weak. Please pray that I would be strong enough to go back to work on Monday.

Tim attended the Jr. High Fine Arts Festival in Troy yesterday and was overwhelmed with love and kindness from those who stopped him to talk to say they were praying for our family. What an incredible prayer network we have! Thank you, thank you, for all who are praying.

We have been blessed to have Sarah here with us for the past two weeks. She has been such a great help to us. Thank you so much, Mike, for letting her be here during this time. Sarah will be traveling home (flying) on Tuesday. Please pray for her safety.

APRIL 26, 2010

"The Lord is good, a strong hold in the day of trouble; and he knoweth them that trust in him." Nahum 1:7

My God knows me! What an awesome thought! As parents, we only want what is good and best for our children. Why should it be any different with God and us? He is our Heavenly Father and always does what is good and best for us, even though we may not understand, we still must trust. He makes no mistakes!

I am very thankful I was able to be back at work today. Thank you so much for all who prayed about that. Hannah came down with the flu this morning after I had already left for work and she has been sick all day. Please pray that the rest of us do not get it, and that she would soon be well. We have all already been exposed, we just need to pray we do not get it.

It is important for me to say it had not even been a year since my last mammogram when I found the lump on my breast. Because of my family history I have had mammograms every year for the last ten years. Nothing showed up on my last three mammograms, yet the doctor thinks I could possibly have had this for more than a year. In other words, mammograms are not the total answer in detecting breast cancer. I cannot stress to you, my friends, how important self-breast exams are. You need to learn how to do them if you don't already know, and be comfortable doing them every month. Do it today! It could save your life. I also want to say that men can get breast cancer. Yes, you read that correctly. Although rare, it is possible. So men, if you find something unusual to your body, go get it checked out.

Here is the 5th point in John Piper's article, "Don't Waste Your Cancer."[6]

5. "You will waste your cancer if you think that 'beating' cancer means staying alive rather than cherishing Christ."

"Satan's and God's designs in your cancer are not the same. Satan designs to destroy your love for Christ. God designs to deepen your love for Christ. Cancer does not win if you die. It wins if you fail to cherish Christ. God's design is to wean you off the breast of the world and feast you on the sufficiency of Christ. It is meant to help you say and feel, 'I count everything as loss because of the surpassing worth of knowing Christ Jesus my Lord.' And to know that therefore, 'To live is Christ, and to die is gain.' Philippians 3:8; 1:21 Cherishing Christ expresses the two core activities of faith: dire need and utter joy. Many psalms cry out in a 'minor key:' we cherish our Savior by needing him to save us from real troubles, real sins, real sufferings, real anguish. Many psalms sing out in a 'major key:' we cherish our Savior by delighting in him, loving him, thanking him for all his benefits to us, rejoicing that his salvation is the weightiest thing in the world and that he gets last say. And many psalms start out in one key and end up in the other. Cherishing Christ is not monochromatic; you live the whole spectrum of human experience with him. To 'bear' cancer is to live knowing how your Father has compassion on his beloved child, because he knows your frame, that you are but dust. Jesus Christ is the way, the truth, and the life. To live is to know him, whom to know is to love."

---

[6] Op. Cit. John Piper

It is my prayer that through this journey I would cherish Christ more.

When you have cancer, sometimes you will feel like you are riding on a rollercoaster, especially in early diagnosis because it seems that everything is happening so quickly. Some days you will be up and some days you will be down. You will have good days and you will have bad days. One day you will be doing just fine and then you will start thinking too far ahead down the road and the "what ifs" will begin creeping up. "What if I have cancer in other parts of my body? What if these treatments don't work? What if my cancer comes back?" And so on. It is a very emotional time and our feelings and emotions can change from day to day, sometimes even hour to hour. This is one reason why it is so important to stay in God's Word every day! God and His Word never change. *"Jesus Christ the same yesterday, and today, and forever."* Hebrews 13:8

One thing I have learned is to take one day at a time and to focus on getting through that day with God's help. Tomorrow will be there waiting for me and God will be there to help carry me through.

APRIL 29, 2010

I want to share with you how God has been answering prayer for us this week! On Monday, Hannah came down with the flu just six days after my first treatment. We prayed that none of us would get it and neither Tim, Sarah nor I got sick. Hannah was over the flu by the next morning. Praise the Lord! Sarah is safe and sound back in Chattanooga with Mike and I have been able to go to work all this week! This afternoon I met with my oncologist and he said my tumor has already begun to shrink some. Wow! This is a huge answer to prayer! My white blood count was within the normal range and I will have my second treatment on Tuesday, May 11. Dr. A said the side effects of my next three chemo treatments should be just the same as this first one and that they would not get any worse as we go along. The side effects of the first treatment were so minimal and much easier than I had anticipated. We were thrilled with this good report as we left the doctor's office today! Thank you so much for all your prayers for us over these past several weeks. It is good to look back and see how God has lead us all the way through each decision and I know He will continue to lead us. That is our desire. We cannot see the path ahead, but we know the One who can! We will be leaving on Wednesday morning to travel to Watertown, WI for several days. All our family will be together again then, along with Tim's parents. I am so thankful I'll be able to make that trip! We are so thankful for answered prayer! The Lord has given me strength through this journey so far and I know He will continue to provide it. *"The Lord is my strength and my shield; my heart trusted in him, and I am helped: therefore my heart greatly rejoiceth; and with my song will I praise him."* Psalm 28:7

MAY 3, 2010

Have you ever been thankful for your eyelashes? I must say, I have never really given my eyelashes much thought. It is one of those things you take for granted and just suppose they will always be there. However, I did thank God for my eyelashes this morning as I was putting my mascara on. It has recently come to my attention, as my hair is beginning to fall out, that very soon I won't have eyelashes, or eyebrows, or any hair for that matter. I guess that won't be all bad....no cleaning hair out of the sink or out of the tub drain after a shower. No shaving or shampooing! Wow! This is going to save me a lot of time in the morning! When I saw my oncologist last week he said I would probably be losing my hair this week. He was right. I am thankful for hats, scarves and wigs. I keep telling Tim I can't wait for him to see me as a redhead!

Hair will grow back, it's not a big deal. I'm hoping mine grows back curly! They say it often does after chemo. Losing your hair--what a small price to pay for getting rid of cancer. Our prayer is that I could be totally healed and totally cancer free. It has been said to us recently that we are now living in the shadow of a mountain. We are praying for God to remove that mountain and to give us the faith to believe that He can remove it. *"If ye have faith as a grain of mustard seed, ye shall say unto this mountain, Remove hence to yonder place; and it shall remove; and nothing shall be impossible unto you."* Matthew 17:20

"With men this is impossible; but with God all things are possible." Matthew 19:26

I am so thankful that I serve a powerful God and that He also is the Great Physician.

MAY 10, 2010

What a wonderful trip we had this past weekend, and how good God has been to our family! He has answered another prayer for us in making it possible for me to make the trip to Wisconsin. We had such a nice time with family and friends and then it was an extra blessing to have all the girls home for the Mother's Day weekend! *"The lines are fallen unto me in pleasant places!"* Psalm 16:6

I am so thankful for the peace that God gives us. I received a card in the mail today and this verse was inside the card: *"Thou wilt keep him in perfect peace, whose mind is stayed on thee: because he trusteth in thee."* Isaiah 26:3 He has given me such peace throughout this journey and I know it is because of your many prayers on our behalf. I have received so many phone calls, messages and cards with words of encouragement and promises of prayers for us. Cards from friends and family, from school children from around the state, and cards from people I don't even know. Wow! What an encouragement to my heart! Tim receives a phone call every Monday from a friend who calls to see how we are doing and tells us he is praying. Thank you for your concern. I do not know how people who do not know the Lord go through times in life like this. What a strength in weakness we who know the Lord as our Savior have to draw on. Our Lord is ever faithful, strong and a source of encouragement through His wonderful Word. I am thankful for this place that I am in right now. Had I not been here I would not have known the wonderful peace of God like I know right now. *"Be careful (anxious) for nothing; but in every thing by prayer and supplication with thanksgiving let your requests be made known unto God. And the peace of God, which passeth all understanding, shall keep your hearts and minds through Christ Jesus."* Philippians 4:6 & 7

I would like to share the 6th point from John Piper's article, "Don't Waste Your Cancer."[7]

6. "You will waste your cancer if you spend too much time reading about cancer and not enough time reading about God."

---

[7] Ibid.

"It is not wrong to know about cancer. Ignorance is not a virtue. But the lure to know more and more and the lack of zeal to know God more and more is symptomatic of unbelief. Cancer is meant to waken us to the reality of God. It is meant to put feeling and force behind the command, "Then shall we know, if we follow on to know the Lord" Hosea 6:3. It is meant to waken us to the truth of Daniel 11:32, "The people that do know their God shall be strong, and do exploits." It is meant to make unshakable, indestructible oak trees out of us: "His delight is in the law of the Lord, and in his law doth he meditate day and night. And he shall be like a tree planted by the rivers of water that bringeth forth his fruit in his season, his leaf also shall not wither; and whatsoever he doeth shall prosper" Psalm 1:2. What a waste of cancer if we read day and night about cancer and not about God.

What is so for your reading is also true for your conversations with others. Other people will often express their care and concern by inquiring about your health. That's good, but the conversation easily gets stuck there. So tell them openly about your sickness, seeking their prayers and counsel, but then change the direction of the conversation by telling them what your God is doing to faithfully sustain you with 10,000 mercies. Robert Murray McCheyne wisely said, "For every one look at your sins, take ten looks at Christ." He was countering our tendency to reverse that 10:1 ratio by brooding over our failings and forgetting the Lord of mercy. What McCheyne says about our sins we can also apply to our sufferings. For every one sentence you say to others about your cancer, say ten sentences about your God, and your hope, and what he is teaching you, and the small blessings of each day. For every hour you spend researching or discussing your cancer, spend ten hours researching and discussing and serving your Lord. Relate all that you are learning about cancer back to Him and His purposes, and you won't become obsessed."

Tomorrow at 1:00 I will have my second treatment. Thank you so much for praying that the treatments will continue to be effective, that the side effects would be minimal and that I would be able to return to work quickly. God is good all the time!

MAY 15, 2010

I feel like I am back in the land of the living today! What a beautiful day in Michigan. I joined Tim outside for a bit and even did a little yard work. We also enjoyed eating lunch in my "secret garden!" My second treatment and the days after was much the same as the first, just as Dr. A said it would be. I cut back a bit this time, however, on the amount of nausea medicine that I took after treatment in order to not be quite as sleepy. It seemed to work pretty well. Even though I slept quite a bit on Thursday and Friday, at least I felt that I could get up some without the struggle of feeling I could not pick my head up off the pillow for more than a few seconds. Thank you so much for all who have been praying for me this week. My next treatment should be on Tuesday, June 1. I should be feeling fine for Hannah's wedding (just thirteen days away)! We are scheduled to leave for Wilmington, NC to visit Rebekah on June 2 at 6:00 a.m. We had made these plans and bought our airline tickets months ago. For my first four treatments I have to go back to the Cancer Center the day after treatment for a shot. This is to boost my white blood count up. The nurses said they could send the shot home after my next treatment, I could take it to Wilmington with me and have someone give it to me there on Wednesday, so we are going ahead with our plans to travel to Wilmington on June 2! We are looking forward to seeing Rebekah's kindergarten class graduate this year and are thanking the Lord for another answer to prayer!

All of us go through difficulties in life--no one is exempt. *"Yet man is born unto trouble, as the sparks fly upward."* Job 5:7 Job himself says in Job 14:1, *"Man that is born of a woman is of few days, and full of trouble."* In John 16:33 Jesus says, *"In the world ye shall have tribulation."* God does not promise us a life without

trial, but His promises are rich with hope. Hope for the believer --
those who by faith have trusted Jesus as their Lord and Savior,
(Romans 6:23, *"For the wages of sin is death; but the gift of God is
eternal life through Jesus Christ our Lord"*) have asked forgiveness
of their sins (Luke 18:13, *"God be merciful to me a sinner"*), and
have asked Him to come into their heart to save them (Romans
10:9, *"That if thou shalt confess with thy mouth the Lord Jesus,
and shalt believe in thine heart that God hath raised him from the
dead, thou shalt be saved"*). He will walk through every
experience with us. He tells us, "I will never leave thee nor
forsake thee." What a comfort!

I am reminded of two things I need to do each day: Trust and
Obey. This is such a great lesson for all of us to learn, and it is so
simple. When I trust God and obey Him, I never need to worry or
fear. When I am trusting Him, I can rest in the truth that He knows
what is best for me and when I am obeying Him I am doing the
things I should be doing. So as we each go through difficult times
throughout life, no matter what those difficulties may be, if we
trust and obey Him it will make our journey sweeter and happier.
"Trust and obey, for there's no other way, to be happy in Jesus,
but to trust and obey!"

MAY 25, 2010

I had an appointment with Dr. A this afternoon and he said my white blood count is back up, my tumor has shrunk a bit more and my next chemo (treatment #3) will be next Tuesday, June 1! Thank you so much for praying! God has answered and it seems as if the treatments are very effective.

Three days now until the wedding! Rebekah gets in late tonight and Mike and Sarah will be coming tomorrow morning. Hannah picks Kyle and Todd up in Detroit tomorrow morning, the rest of Kyle's family will drive in tomorrow evening and Tim's parents and one brother fly in tomorrow night. The rest of the wedding party and the rest of our family will be coming on Thursday. Please pray for Tim tonight. He has not been feeling well today and is in great pain with a migraine headache right now. I'm thinking stress... (Note to self: do not ever try replacing your bathroom floor the week of your daughter's wedding. There is just not enough time to get everything finished with all this company coming...)

What a great 5K race my friends had on Saturday! They finished in just thirty three minutes and God held the rain off until they were on the way home! I wish I could have been there. It must have been an incredible experience! Thank you again, Ladies, for your love and support. One of my nieces is also raising funds for the cure and will be participating in a 3-day, sixty mile walk in Washington, DC in October. Thank you for your support.

I am so thankful for God's Word. When I am discouraged, it encourages and comforts me. Just this morning I was reading in Psalm 71, and verses 19-21 were of great comfort to me. *"Thy righteousness also, O God, is very high, who hast done great things: O God, who is like unto thee! Thou, which hast shewed me great and sore troubles shalt quicken me again, and shalt bring me up again from the depths of the earth. Thou shalt increase my greatness, and comfort me on every side."*

God is good all the time.

JUNE 1, 2010

Isn't it amazing how quickly your life can change directions in just one day? I never would have imagined even three months ago that I would be having chemotherapy treatments for breast cancer all summer. I am so thankful that my cancer was no surprise to my Heavenly Father. He had it all planned out before the creation of the world. I will trust and rest in His wisdom.

Three treatments down, thirteen more to go! My treatment went well today. I actually fell asleep for a short time while I was there! I think it was just sitting down and relaxing for more than ten minutes that did it -- something I have not really done in over a week! What a busy week it was, but what a great week! It was so good to have so much of our family here. The wedding went off without a hitch--what a beautiful bride Hannah Joy was and what a fun time we all had! And, God gave us beautiful weather all weekend so we could enjoy a picnic here in our backyard on Saturday with all our family and Kyle's family that was still here. Thank you, again, for all who were praying about these things. Hannah and Kyle made it safely to Connecticut and Kyle is now back to work and Hannah is busy unpacking and getting things put away.

Lord willing, Tim and I will leave at 6:00 am tomorrow for our trip to Wilmington. Please pray that I would not get too tired or sick this time especially. We will be attending Rebekah's K-5 class graduation and then Rebekah has some special things planned for Saturday and Sunday. Also, Tim will be preaching at their church on Sunday evening. We will be traveling home next Monday.

Let me share point seven from John Piper's article, "Don't Waste

Your Cancer."[8]

7. "You will waste your cancer if you let it drive you into solitude instead of deepen your relationships with manifest affection."

"When Epaphroditus brought the gifts to Paul sent by the Philippian church he became ill and almost died. Paul tells the Philippians, 'For he longed after you all and was full of heaviness, because that ye had heard that he had been sick' (Phil. 2:26-27). What an amazing response! It does not say they were distressed that he was sick, but that he was distressed because they heard he was sick. That is the kind of heart God is aiming to create with cancer: a deeply affectionate, caring heart for people. Don't waste your cancer by retreating into yourself. Our culture is terrified of facing death. It is obsessed with medicine. It idolizes youth, health and energy. It tries to hide any signs of weakness or imperfection. You will bring huge blessing to others by living openly, believingly and lovingly within your weaknesses. Paradoxically, moving out into relationships when you are hurting and weak will actually strengthen others. 'One anothering' is a two-way street of generous giving and grateful receiving. Your need gives others an opportunity to love. And since love is always God's highest purpose in you, too, you will learn his finest and most joyous lessons as you find small ways to express concern for others even when you are most weak. A great, life-threatening weakness can prove amazingly freeing. Nothing is left for you to do except to be loved by God and others, and to love God and others."

I know God is going to use my cancer journey in the weeks,

---

[8] Ibid.

months and years ahead to let me share with and minister to others who are going through the same thing. This is one of the reasons I believe God allowed me to have cancer: so I can be a help to others. II Corinthians 1:4, *"Who comforteth us in all our tribulation, that we may be able to comfort them which are in any trouble, by the comfort wherewith we ourselves are comforted of God."* I can say, I have felt your love, your prayers, your concern and your care for my family and I, and for that I am deeply touched and so thankful. I am humbled.

God is so good!

JUNE 10, 2010

This has been an incredible journey that God has placed me on. While it is not something I would have chosen for myself, I am thankful for it and also thankful for those of you who are walking along side, praying for me and encouraging me along the way. Over the past three months I have learned much of God's peace, His grace and His love. He has drawn me closer to his side and I believe has given me a more tender, compassionate heart. God knew I needed more compassion for people who are going through physical difficulties. I want to learn the things He is teaching me through this journey and I want to come through it a more godly person.

I have learned to appreciate each day more and more and I know that every day is a gift. James 1:17, *"Every good gift and every perfect gift is from above, and cometh down from the Father of lights, with whom is no variableness, neither shadow of turning."* None of us knows if we will be here tomorrow and so we need to focus on today. James tells us in James 4:14 & 15 *"Whereas ye know not what shall be on the morrow. For what is your life? It is even a vapour, that appeareth for a little time, and then vanisheth away. For that ye ought to say, If the Lord will, we shall live, and do this or that."* It is only if God wills that we will be here tomorrow. I am comforted by that because His will is always best.

We had a great trip to Wilmington and a wonderful visit with Rebekah and Heather (Rebekah's roommate). I was able to sleep a good bit on Wednesday on the plane and then on Thursday I slept most of the day at Rebekah's house. By Thursday night I was feeling fine and able to go and enjoy the K-5 graduation and on Friday we spent most of the day at school. It was the last day of school and there were awards given out in the classroom in the morning and then we went outside to the playground for the party. We got to eat and visit with the students and their parents for a long time and that was a blessing. One of my favorite things to do is to walk on the beach and we did that two evenings and also went out for seafood two times! On Saturday morning we

toured the USS North Carolina and then in the afternoon had lunch at the Wilmington Tea Room -- Tea by the Sea! What a treat that was! Sunday was church, out for dinner, a nap and then Tim presented "Stories in Stones" in the evening service at Grace. After church Rebekah had invited friends over and we had some good fellowship and then after they left, Rebekah, Heather, Tim and I played the Wii until my arm was sore! We stayed up late since it was our last night there and we were having such a good time. On Monday I slept most of the way home on the planes. Thankfully I had Tuesday off work, and then went back to work on Wednesday. We really had no down time after the wedding until we got home on Monday night. Then it hit us. Everyone was gone. It was just the two of us. We have an empty nest. Again. I walked into Hannah's room and cried. It is not that I don't like empty nest. I really love it. It is the change I don't like. I don't do well with change and never have. It is an adjustment, and it gets better every day. I'm sure in another day or two things will be great! :)

Recently Satan has tried to discourage me by getting me to think too far ahead. "What if after I am cancer free, my cancer comes back in my bones, my brain, my liver or my lungs?" "After all, I do have Stage 3 cancer and it is already in my lymph nodes." "Will I live to see my grandchildren?" I have to keep telling myself to take one day at a time and to focus on all the good and all the answered prayer God has given us thus far. He is good, He controls all things, He knows all about me, even the number of hairs on my head (not many right now!), and He knows about my tomorrows. Lord, help me to trust your promises when I get discouraged and to know you hold the future, and help me to take one day at a time.

Tim and I went out and played tennis this afternoon after I got off work. It felt great! We didn't play long, but we got out there and did it! Tennis is something Tim and I have enjoyed doing together ever since we were fifteen years old! Lord willing, we will be doing that much more this summer. It is much harder than Wii tennis!

God has been so good and has allowed me to already make it through (and not just make it through, but really enjoy each event and feel great while doing it! PTL!) three of the four major things we had planned for this spring/summer. My mom's 90th birthday party in Alaska is the next thing. We purchased our airline tickets months ago and are scheduled to leave on July 27. The thing is, at that time I will be receiving my treatments every week. It will be a different chemo with different side effects than what I have now. I have one more treatment on this chemo on June 22 and then three weeks after that I begin the new chemo every week for twelve weeks. Please pray that the doctor will allow me to go an extra day between treatments, or that He would work out all the details for this trip. I need to take one day at a time. I will be talking with Dr. A about this next week at my appointment.

Philippians 4:6 *"Be careful [anxious] for nothing; but in every thing by prayer and supplication with thanksgiving let your requests be made known unto God. And the peace of God, which passeth all understanding, shall keep your hearts and minds through Christ Jesus."*

JUNE 15, 2010

THANK YOU FOR PRAYING!

I have some more answers to prayer that I would like to share with you! I had an appointment with my oncologist, Dr. A, today and he said it would not be a problem for me to go to Alaska! He also said my tumor is continuing to shrink, although not as much this time. I am so thankful the chemo is doing its job! My next treatment will be next Tuesday, June 22. This will be treatment #4 and the last treatment of this chemo (A & C).

I want to give God the glory for what He has done and I also want to thank each of you who have prayed for these specific things! Specific requests get specific results/answers.

I feel so blessed to have so many people praying for me. People I don't even know are praying for me. Wow! God bless each one.

God has given me the strength to do just about everything I normally do or would do, had I not had cancer. He has given extra strength during extremely busy times for me this spring. Some say this is amazing. I say I serve an amazing God! He can still answer prayers and still do miracles. We have seen Him answer so many prayers for us and He is always good. He would still be good had He not answered the way we wanted. I fully intend to live my life as long as I am feeling well and I believe that is what God would want me to do. Why should I sit around when there are tennis games to play, bikes to ride and strawberries to pick? I want to stay strong. I want to fight like a girl! The doctors told me to live my life and my body will tell me when to slow down if I listen to it. I am not afraid to take a nap if I need to.

I have shared this before, but I would like to share it again. I have had several people share this with me over the past few months and it comforts me every time:

"First, He brought me here. It is by His will I am in this strait place: in that fact I will rest.
Next, He will keep me here in His love, and give me grace to behave as His child.
Then, He will make the trial a blessing, teaching me the lessons He intends me to learn, and working in me the grace He means to bestow.
Last, in His good time He can bring me out again - how and when He knows.

Let me say I am here,
1) By God's appointment,
2) In His Keeping,
3) Under his training,
4) For His Time."

--Andrew Murray[9]

---

[9] Op Cit. Andrew Murray

JULY 8, 2010

"Blessed be the Lord, who daily loadeth us with benefits, even the God of our salvation." Psalm 68:19

"Bless the Lord, O my soul, and forget not all his benefits; Who forgiveth all thine iniquities; who healeth all thy diseases;" Psalm 103:2&3.

God has done so much for me and given me so much more than what I deserve! He has given me promises from His Word to cling to that are of such comfort. What would I do without Him?

I have finished my chemo treatments with the drugs Doxorubicin (Adriamycin, Adria) and Cytoxan (Cyclophosphamide), (also known as "A C") and will start chemo treatment with Paclitaxel (Taxol), (also known as "T") this next Monday, July 12. This will be given every week for twelve weeks. The side effects from "T" are different than "A C." The doctor tells me I shouldn't have nausea/vomiting this time, (it is uncommon) but Taxol can affect the nervous system causing a number of symptoms. I may also experience muscle and joint pain for two or three days after each treatment. Please pray specifically that I would not have a reaction to this drug (as some do), that the chemo would be effective in killing the cancer cells and that the side effects would be minimal. These treatments will take me through the end of September and then my surgery will most likely be sometime in October.

Tim and I had a fun 4th of July weekend--went to the parade in Fenton on Saturday morning, picnic with friends in Clarkston Saturday afternoon and then back to Fenton for fireworks

Saturday night. Sunday we were at two different churches--First Baptist Church of Clarkston in the morning and then Maranatha Baptist Church in Flint in the evening. What a blessing to see so many dear friends and to have so many tell us they have been praying for us. My heart is so blessed!! Then on Monday we packed up the van and headed out, had a picnic lunch, went to a baseball game Monday evening and stayed at a cute Bed & Breakfast that evening. The name of it was The Little Purple House. On Tuesday we slept in, shopped and spent quality time together and took our time coming home. Thanks, Honey, for a nice getaway!

I would like to share point eight from the article "Don't Waste Your Cancer"[10] by John Piper:

8. "You will waste your cancer if you grieve as those who have no hope."

---

[10] Op. Cit. John Piper

"Paul used this phrase in relation to those whose loved ones had died: But I would not have you to be ignorant, brethren, concerning them which are asleep, that ye sorrow not, even as others which have no hope.' (1 Thessalonians 4:13). There is a grief at death. Even for the believer who dies, there is temporary loss--loss of body, and loss of loved ones here, and loss of earthly ministry. But the grief is different--it is permeated with hope. 'willing rather to be absent from the body, and to be present with the Lord' (2 Corinthians 5:8). Don't waste your cancer grieving as those who don't have this hope. Show the world this different way of grieving. Paul said that he would have had 'grief upon grief' if his friend Epaphroditus had died. He had been grieving, feeling the painful weight of his friend's illness. He would have doubly grieved if his friend had died. But this loving, honest, God-oriented grief coexisted with 'rejoice always' and 'the peace of God that passes understanding' and 'showing a genuine concern for your welfare.' How on earth can heartache coexist with love, joy, peace, and an indestructible sense of life purpose? In the inner logic of faith, this makes perfect sense. In fact, because you have hope, you may feel the sufferings of this life more keenly: grief upon grief. In contrast, the grieving that has no hope often chooses denial or escape of busyness because it can't face reality without becoming distraught. In Christ, you know what's at stake, and so you keenly feel the wrong of this fallen world. You don't take pain and death for granted. You love what is good, and hate what is evil. After all, you follow in the image of 'a man of sorrows, acquainted with grief.' But this Jesus chose his cross willingly 'for the joy set before him.' He lived and died in hopes that all come true. His pain was not muted by denial or medication, nor was it tainted with despair, fear, or thrashing about for any straw of hope that might change his circumstances. Jesus' final promises overflow with the gladness of solid hope amid sorrows: 'My joy will be in you, and your joy will be made full. Your grief will be turned to joy. No one will take your joy away from you. Ask, and you will receive, so that your joy will be made full. These things I speak in the world, so that they may have my joy made full in themselves.' (selection from John 15-17)"

What a blessed hope we as Christians have! "It's hard to lose a loved one to the grave, but we have the blessed hope that Jesus gave, God shall wipe all the tears from our eyes, when we meet in that land beyond the skies! Heaven is sounding sweeter all the time, seems like lately it's always on my mind, someday I'll leave this world behind, Heaven sounding sweeter all the time!" Life is short and death is certain. I have three friends, all women, who have passed from this world into the next in the past two weeks (they say death comes in threes, and it's funny how that happens so often). None of us knows when our time on earth will be finished, but we can know where we will spend eternity. God wants us to spend it in Heaven with Him, but we must choose. By not accepting Him, we are choosing to reject Him. As a twelve year old girl I chose to accept Him into my heart and life and I am so glad I did. Romans 10:9-13 says, *"That if thou shalt confess with thy mouth the Lord Jesus, and shalt believe in thine heart that God hath raised him from the dead, thou shalt be saved. For with the heart man believeth unto righteousness; and with the mouth confession is made unto salvation. For the scripture saith, Whosoever believeth on him shall not be ashamed. For there is no difference between the Jew and the Greek: for the same Lord over all is rich unto all that call upon him. For whosoever shall call upon the name of the Lord shall be saved."* I would hate to think where my life would be now had I not made that decision. He has led me all the way! Thank you, Father! If you are reading this and have never asked Jesus to save you from your sins and take you to

Sue Schmig

Heaven when you die, won't you please do it now?

JULY 12, 2010

Just a quick update on today:

Dr. A's office called today to see if I could come in at 9:30 instead of noon, so my appointment got moved up. We met with Dr. A first and then I had chemo right after that. Dr. A said my white blood count was good and that my tumor continues to shrink. That is great news! There was no reaction to the new chemo and I am very thankful for that. When we got to the chemo treatment room we saw Harold & Frieda who had just gotten there for Harold's treatment so we sat next to them and got to visit for several hours and that was a special treat! We are chemo buddies now! Then about halfway through our treatments, another friend, Jim, came in to have his blood drawn so we got to visit with him also. Friends with common blessings/trials. Friends I pray for every day and I know they pray for me as well. I am thankful for the common bond we share and what a blessing to see them and spend time with them today! Thank you, Lord.

One of the medications they gave me to prevent any reaction made me very sleepy and I came home and took a two and a half hour nap. I will have eleven more treatments and they will be every week now. That will take me through the end of September and then my surgery will most likely be in October.

We are enjoying a nice visit with Tim's dad and brother who are here from Wisconsin & Minnesota. They came to remodel our bathroom for us (since we don't know how!) They got in on Friday night.

Thank you so much for praying for us. We appreciate it more than you know!

"Continue in prayer, and watch in the same with thanksgiving: Withal praying also for us, that God would open unto us a door of utterance, to speak the mystery of Christ, for which I am also in bonds: That I may make it manifest as I ought to speak."
Colosssians 4: 2-4

JULY 26, 2010

Tim and I leave tomorrow for Alaska! We are going to visit my mom and celebrate her 90th birthday with her. Her party will be on Saturday. I'm looking forward to seeing my mom, Rebekah & Heather, my sister and her family and my brother, along with a lot of my mom's friends.

God has been so good to me in allowing me to make this trip. He knew the desires of my heart and has answered prayers in a way I would have never imagined and I am so thankful!

I had my 7th chemo today and it went well. My chemo buddy, Harold, arrived shortly after we got there, so they sat next to us and we got to visit with Harold & Frieda today as we had our treatments. We also saw Jim again today for a short while. After my next chemo next Tuesday I will be half done with my chemo treatments! The time is really going by quickly.

Here is point nine from John Piper's article, "Don't Waste Your Cancer:"[11]

9. "You will waste your cancer if you treat sin as casually as before."

"Are your besetting sins as attractive as they were before you had cancer? If so you are wasting your cancer. Cancer is designed to destroy the appetite for sin. Pride, greed, lust, hatred, unforgiveness, impatience, laziness, procrastination--all these are the adversaries that cancer is meant to attack. Don't just think of battling against cancer. Also think of battling with cancer. All

---

[11] Ibid.

these things are worse enemies than cancer. Don't waste the power of cancer to crush these foes. Let the presence of eternity make the sins of time look as futile as they really are. "For what shall it profit a man, if he shall gain the whole world and lose his own soul?' Mark 8:36

Suffering really is meant to wean you from sin and strengthen your faith. If you are God-less, then suffering magnifies sin. Will you become more bitter, despairing, addictive, fearful, frenzied, avoidant, sentimental, godless in how you go about life? Will you pretend it's business as usual? Will you come to terms with death, on your terms? But if you are God's, then suffering in Christ's hands will change you, always slowly, sometimes quickly. You come to terms with life and death on his terms. He will gently purify you, cleanse you of vanities. He will make you need him and love him. He rearranges your priorities, so first things come first more often. He will walk with you. Of course you'll fail at times, perhaps seized by irritability or brooding, escapism or fears. But he will always pick you up when you stumble. Your inner enemy - a moral cancer 10,000 times more deadly than your physical cancer - will be dying as you continue seeking and finding your Savior."

Tonight I am rejoicing in answered prayer and thanking God for teaching me more about His goodness and His love. I pray I never treat sin in a casual way, as the world does.

"Wherefore seeing we also are compassed about with so great a cloud of witnesses, let us lay aside every weight, and the sin which doth so easily beset us, and let us run with patience the race that is set before us, Looking unto Jesus the author and finished of our faith; who for the joy that was set before him endured the cross, despising the shame, and is set down at the right hand of the throne of God. For consider him that endured such contradiction

of sinners against himself, lest ye be wearied and faint in your minds." Hebrews 12:1-3

AUGUST 14, 2010

It was a great trip to Alaska celebrating my mom's 90th birthday and I am very thankful to have been able to make the trip. For the most part I have been feeling great and have had no major side effects since starting this new weekly chemo. I now have completed nine treatments and just have seven more to go. God has answered so many prayers for us over these past several months! Thank you for all your prayers!

We are thrilled to know our first grandchild is on the way! What an exciting time for Mike & Sarah and for all of us! Today when I was out shopping I just couldn't help myself when I walked by the baby clothes! This baby is going to be very well dressed that's for sure!

Here is the last point from the article I've been sharing:

10.[12] "You will waste your cancer if you fail to use it as a means of witness to the truth and glory of Christ."

"Christians are never anywhere by divine accident. There are reasons for why we wind up where we do. Consider what Jesus said about painful, unplanned circumstances: 'But before all these, they shall lay their hands on you, and persecute you, delivering you up to the synagogues, and into prisons, being brought before kings and rulers for my name's sake. And it shall turn to you for a testimony.' (Luke 21:12-13). So it is with cancer. This will be an opportunity to bear witness. Christ is infinitely worthy. Here is a golden opportunity to show that He is worth more than life. Don't waste it.

Jesus is your life. He is the man before whom every knee will bow. He has defeated death once for all. He will finish what He has begun. Let your light so shine as you live in Him, by Him, through Him, for Him. In your cancer, you will need your brothers and sisters in Christ to witness to the truth and glory of Christ, to walk with you, to live out their faith beside you, to love you. And you can do the same with them and with all others, becoming the heart that loves with the love of Christ, the mouth filled with hope to both friends and strangers. Remember, you are not left alone. You will have the help you need. 'But my God shall supply all your need according to His riches in glory by Christ Jesus' (Philippians 4:19)."

I am so thankful we can encourage each other in the Lord. You all have been such an encouragement to me over these past several

---

[12] Ibid.

months, and I pray I can return that back to you in some small way. We need each other. I do not know how the unsaved world can go through difficulties of life without God and the strength, comfort, grace and peace that only He can give. I am so blessed.

Tomorrow I am going with Tim as he will be speaking at two different churches. Immanuel Baptist Church in Corunna in the morning and Dixie Baptist Church in Clarkston in the evening. I am looking forward to seeing many of our good friends!

September 21, 2010

God is good all the time. I know this is true, but sometimes I need to repeat it out loud to myself. It is good to say it. He always knows what is best. One more chemo treatment next Tuesday and then an appointment with the surgeon on Wednesday to hopefully set up my surgery. Please pray that I would be able to have the surgery as soon as possible after my last chemo. Thank you so much for the prayers that have gone up for me over these past almost six months. I cannot begin to tell you what they have meant to me.

God is teaching me to hate sin in a way I have never hated it before. Sin hurts people and destroys families and lives. I never want to treat sin in a casual manner. Our world is so full of sin and wickedness and it lures us and tempts us to "eat, drink and be merry." For the born-again Christian, this world is not our home. Lord, remind me that I am a pilgrim. I am just passing through, my treasures are laid up somewhere beyond the blue, the angels beckon me from Heaven's open door, and I can't feel at home in this world anymore! Satan wants to attack us and tempt us and get our eyes off what we should be focusing on and put them on the things of this world. We are told in I John 2:15-17 *"Love not the world, neither the things that are in the world. If any man love the world, the love of the Father is not in him. For all that is in the world, the lust of the flesh, and the lust of the eyes, and the pride of life, is not of the Father, but is of the world. And the world passeth away, and the lust thereof: but he that doeth the will of God abideth for ever."* And then in James 1:13-15 we are *told "Let no man say when he is tempted, I am tempted of God: for God cannot be tempted with evil, neither tempteth he any man: But every man is tempted, when he is drawn away of his own lust, and enticed. Then when lust hath conceived, it bringeth forth sin: and sin, when it is finished, bringeth forth death."* Lust and sin will cloud our thinking. That is why it is so important to stay in the Book and do right so we can have God's way of thinking. Our opinions don't matter, but what matters is written in black and white. I love that. Maybe that is why I am a black and white kind of gal. Have you been in the Book today? What is God teaching you?

When lust and sin enter in, and when the Holy Spirit works in our hearts and convicts us, it will produce guilt. We are living in a world that says guilt is a bad thing for us to feel. Do not buy into that lie. It comes straight from the pits of Hell and Satan wants you to believe that lie. If you feel guilt from sin, you need to get down on your knees and ask God for forgiveness from the sin that has caused that guilt. The world says, "no guilt, no sin." Listen to these statements taken from the book The Vanishing Conscience [13]-- drawing the line in a No-Fault, Guilt-Free World that I am reading: "No guilt and no sin -- that kind of thinking has all but driven words like sin, repentance, contrition, atonement, restitution, and redemption out of public discourse. If no one is supposed to feel guilty, how could anyone be a sinner? Modern culture has the answer: people are *victims*. Victims are not responsible for what they do; they are casualties of what happens to them. So every human failing must be described in terms of how the perpetrator has been victimized. We are all supposed to be "sensitive" and "compassionate" enough to see that the very behaviors we used to label "sin" are actually evidence of victimization."

---

[13] The Vanishing Conscience by John MacArthur 2005

To say, 'follow your heart' is no advice a Christian should be giving. We should instead advise, follow God and His leading! *"The heart is deceitful above all things, and desperately wicked: who can know it?"* Jeremiah 17:9 My heart is heavy and broken for those who do not see sin as God sees it. Only God can change a mind and a heart and so tonight I continue to weep and pray.

Lord, help us all to see sin as you see it and not to treat it casually.

OCTOBER 5, 2010

Just a quick update tonight. Well, since the last time I wrote I have finished all my chemo treatments! Sixteen treatments over twenty four weeks and they are all behind me now! God gave me amazing strength and health through that part of my journey and allowed me to keep working at my job through all of it. We were even able to make all of the trips that we had planned for this spring and summer. I did not suffer the side effects that I was told I may. I have stayed healthy with good white blood counts through all of it. In fact, last Monday, the day before my last chemo, when I met with my oncologist he said to me, "I would never know you were on chemo because your white blood counts are so good." My God did that and He is the God of the impossible! These are answers to prayers! On my last day of chemo, last Tuesday, just before we left, the nurses brought me balloons and a "certificate of achievement" for finishing all my chemo and they had hugs for us as we left. One said to me, "your girls would be proud of you." (All of our girls were with me for my first chemo in April.) It was an emotional time.

My appointment with the surgeon that was scheduled for last Wednesday got rescheduled for next week. My oncologist wanted me to have another MRI first so they could see how much the tumor has shrunk. So now I'm just waiting to see the surgeon and to get my surgery scheduled. With God's help I am ready to begin the next phase of this journey! Please pray that I could stay healthy and that the surgery can be scheduled as soon as possible. I won't know if I have to have any radiation treatments until after what is found during the surgery.

This October is the 25th Anniversary of National Breast Cancer Awareness Month. Interesting fact: although rare, about 440 men die of breast cancer every year (in comparison, over 40,000 women die of breast cancer each year). Breast cancer is 100 times more common in women than in men. According to the American Cancer Society (ACS), an estimated 192,370 new cases of invasive breast cancer are expected to have been diagnosed among women in the United States after 2009's findings are totaled. Additionally, the ACS predicts that approximately 1,910 new cases will have been found in men during 2009. The ACS also reports that an estimated 40,610 breast cancer deaths are expected to have occurred in 2009 (40,170 women; 440 men). To those thousands of people across our nation who have been affected by breast cancer in some way, shape, or form, I would like to commend your courage, strength and hopefully, faith, in the face of hardships both won and lost.

I want to thank my friend Leigh Ann and the Lake Orion Baptist School girls volleyball team for their prayers and support especially during the month of October. This month they are wearing pink ribbons, pink nail polish and pink shoe laces during all their games and praying for me and for two other ladies that are battling this horrible disease that we call breast cancer. My heart is deeply touched that they would do this for us. My heart is also deeply touched that so many of you have told me you are praying for me every day. I am humbled and I am blessed. God has answered your prayers.

OCTOBER 21, 2010

"Thou wilt keep him in perfect peace, whose mind is stayed on thee." Isaiah 26:3

I am about to begin the next phase of my journey and God has given me such wonderful peace. I have no fear about tomorrow and am resting in His love and peace. I want to keep my focus on Him and what He has done. That is when He gives peace. His Word is such a comfort.

My surgery will be at 10:00 tomorrow morning and we have to be at the hospital at 8:00. Please pray for Dr. V as he operates, that God would guide his hands and give him wisdom during the surgery. Also please pray for a good recovery with no complications. I will probably only be in the hospital until Sunday, but I will be off work for several weeks. Thanks, Tim and Sarah, for being here for me. I love you!

I am so thankful for the prayers of God's people on my behalf. They have encouraged me in so many ways and helped me along this journey. Thank you dear Friends!

In closing, let me share two verses that I have claimed as my own during these past few months. Again, a reminder of God's wonderful peace. *"Be careful (anxious) for nothing; but in every thing by prayer and supplication with thanksgiving let your requests be made known unto God. And the peace of God, which passeth all understanding, shall keep your hearts and minds through Christ Jesus."* Philippians 4:6 & 7.

OCTOBER 28, 2010

"He shall call upon me, and I will answer him: I will be with him in trouble; I will deliver him, and honour him. With long life will I satisfy him, and shew him my salvation." Psalm 91:15 & 16

Yesterday was a day we had prayed for and we are rejoicing in God's answer! Sometimes God answers yes and sometimes He answers no. He is always good no matter what His answer is. I trust that if His answer had been no, I would still be rejoicing in His answer because He is good all the time and His plan is always perfect. Had He answered no, I know His grace and comfort would have been sufficient to carry my family and I through even unto death.

We had our follow-up visit with the surgeon yesterday morning and when we left we were rejoicing and grinning from ear to ear! We may have shed a few joyful tears as well! Ever since we began this journey we have prayed for complete healing from the cancer, always understanding that He may have other plans for me and if He did, then that was ok too. The pathology report came back showing no evidence of any cancer in the fourteen lymph nodes and breast tissue that was removed! In fact, Dr. V said the pathologist called him to ask him exactly what it was he was supposed to be looking for because he could find no cancer cells at all! This is a miracle! The doctors will credit this to the chemotherapy. I give all the glory and credit to my Great Physician! He alone has power to heal! My God is a God of miracles and I believe He still performs them today. I also believe God performed a miracle in my body by healing me of my cancer. Without Him we can do nothing! The power of life and death are in His hands! Glory to God!

The oncologist will determine whether or not I will have any radiation treatments after I am totally healed up from the surgery and we will go back to see him in about three weeks.

I was so thankful to have my surgery so quickly after my last chemo. God's timing was just perfect once again. Sarah was able to come up from Chattanooga to be with us for a week during the surgery/recovery and what a blessing she was to us. The job she has allows her to work from her computer wherever she is, so she was able to work some while she was here as well. The surgery went very well with no complications and Tim and Sarah were surrounded by close friends as they waited for the surgery to be over. We were initially told I would only be in the hospital one night. We thought that was crazy! I am thankful for my friend Donna who stayed with me after everyone else had gone home. My surgery was Friday morning and I ended up coming home on Sunday afternoon. The pain was managed very well with morphine while I was at the hospital and then Vicodin once I came home. God has given me a very high pain tolerance and so, I really didn't experience much pain at all after the first two days. I am off the pain meds completely now.

While we were at the hospital we met a young lady who is very ill and just starting chemo. On Saturday morning while we were taking a walk down the hall she was standing at her door and asked me where I had gotten my hat. She told us she will soon be losing her hair. We had a chance to talk with her a bit and Tim and Sarah went out later that day and bought her a hat at Katie's Spa in Lapeer. This is the place I got my wig and all my hats. We took it to her later that afternoon and also gave her a tract. Please pray for Marina. We exchanged phone numbers and I am hoping to talk with her again soon.

It is wonderful to be home and resting well in my own bed! The hospital was ok, but why do they have to wake you up every hour during the night? There's no place like home and naps are wonderful! I want to make a full recovery from the surgery and so while we were at the doctor yesterday I asked him about when I can drive and when I can go out, etc. He said not to overdo it, but if I am feeling up to it, it should be fine. Listen to my body. After we got our wonderful news yesterday, I really wanted to be at church last night. So, I came home after we went out for my birthday lunch and took a nap and then we went to church last night. I told my family there was nowhere else I would have rather been last night than in church praising God for what He has done in my life! It was good to share what God had done. I know some may think I should have been home in bed, but there is plenty of time for that and I promise not to overdo it and to get plenty of rest in the weeks ahead. Today I am resting and rejoicing in what God has done and my heart is overflowing!

Thank you once again, dear Friends, for the many prayers for us and for the many words of encouragement you have shared with me over these months. What a blessing you have been! *"I thank my God upon every remembrance of you."* Philippians 1:3

DECEMBER 20, 2010

"The Lord hath done great things for us; whereof we are glad."
Psalm 126:3

2010 was a year filled with great challenges and great blessings. As the year began I never would have dreamed that in a few short months I would be diagnosed with stage three breast cancer that had spread to my lymph nodes and that I would go through twenty four weeks of chemotherapy and then surgery with a six-week recovery time. As I look back I can see how God calmed the storm in my heart after just learning my news, just as He calmed the storm at sea in Mark 4. In that passage He used His words "Peace, be still" to calm the waters. Over the past months He has used His Word many times over to calm the storm in my heart. He is with us through all our storms in life no matter what they may be. He cares for us and is a compassionate and loving God!

When we began this journey back in March, we begin to pray for several specific requests. We prayed that the chemo would be effective in killing all the cancer cells in my body. We asked God to help us be a testimony and to use this trial in our lives to encourage others. Then we also prayed for complete healing.

After meeting with a radiology oncologist at the University of Michigan Hospital in Ann Arbor, it was decided that I would not need to go through any radiation treatments. I had a complete response to the chemotherapy. (The doctors tell me this is quite rare!) We know God did this and that He chose to answer the many specific prayers that have gone up on my behalf! All praise to God, I am now cancer-free! God has given me complete healing and we are rejoicing in His goodness! My hair is growing back and to my delight it is coming in curly! This is a special blessing from the Lord!

As I end this journey I want to thank each of you for walking with me, encouraging me, supporting me, loving me and praying for me and for my family. What a blessing you have been to my heart and to my life. So many times you said just the right thing at just the right time, or shared a verse that encouraged me just when I needed it. I am humbled and I am grateful.

I have learned so much from this journey God placed me on and the most important lesson I learned is that Every Day is A Gift!

Our first grandchild born in March of 2011

ABOUT THE AUTHOR

Since 1980 Sue has been blessed to be married to the love of her life, Tim, and they live in an older home in the Historic Mason district of Owosso, Michigan. They have three adult daughters, two sons-in-law and four wonderful grandchildren. Sue enjoys knitting, gardening, bike riding, playing tennis and traveling.

Sue has been cancer free since October 2010 and since that time has been able to minister to other ladies who have experienced the cancer journey. Her prayer is that this book will encourage those who are going through difficult trials in their lives. You may contact Sue at storiesinstones868@gmail.com

Made in the USA
Columbia, SC
20 August 2018